SIDE by SIDE

HANDBOOK of
TEACHING STRATEGIES

Steven J. Molinsky
Bill Bliss

Longman

Side by Side Handbook of Teaching Strategies
© 2000 by Addison Wesley Longman, Inc.

Pearson Education
10 Bank St.
White Plains, NY 10606

Editorial director: *Allen Ascher*
Director of design and production: *Rhea Banker*
Associate director of electronic production: *Aliza Greenblatt*
Production manager: *Ray Keating*
Senior manufacturing manager: *Patrice Fraccio*
Manufacturing buyer: *Dave Dickey*
Electronic production editor, page compositor, interior designer: *Paula D. Williams*

The authors gratefully acknowledge the contribution of Tina Carver in the development
of the *Side by Side* program.

ISBN 0-13-026371-0

Printed in the United States of America

10   9   8   7   6   5   4   3

CONTENTS

INTRODUCTION

Strategies for Presenting, Practicing, and Reviewing
Guided Conversation Lessons

Relating Lesson Content to Students' Lives and Experiences

Options for Additional Practice

Side by Side Communication Activities

INTRODUCTION

The *Side by Side Handbook of Teaching Strategies* is designed to serve as a resource for maximizing use of the *Side by Side* textbook series. More than 75 interactive activities for reinforcing grammar structures and vocabulary from the texts are presented. Although each activity is illustrated by an example from a specific lesson in the series, you should feel free to adapt these activities for any lessons where you feel they would be appropriate. In addition, strategies for presenting, practicing, and reviewing guided conversation lessons and exercises are offered. These lessons constitute the core of the *Side by Side* approach to active, dynamic language learning.

Strategies for Presenting, Practicing, and Reviewing Guided Conversation Lessons

The Guided Conversation Methodology

Side by Side offers learners of English a dynamic, communicative approach to learning the language. Through the methodology of guided conversations, *Side by Side* engages students in meaningful conversational exchanges within carefully structured grammatical frameworks, and then encourages students to break away from the textbook and *use* these frameworks to create conversations on their own. All the language practice that is generated through the texts results in active communication between students . . . practicing speaking together "side by side."

Model conversations serve as the vehicles for introducing new grammatical structures and many communicative uses of English. Since the model becomes the basis for all the exercises that follow, it is essential that students be given sufficient practice with it before proceeding with the lesson.

In the numbered exercises that follow the model, students pair up and work "side by side," placing new content into the given conversational framework. These exercises form the core learning activity of each conversation lesson.

Introducing Model Conversations

Given the importance of the model conversation, it is essential that students practice it several times in a variety of ways before going on to the exercises.

The *Teacher's Guide* offers the following comprehensive eight-step approach to introducing the model:

1. Have students look at the model illustration. This helps establish the context of the conversation.

2. Set the scene.

3. *Present the model.* With books closed, have students listen as you present the model or play the tape one or more times. To make the presentation of the model as realistic as

possible, you might draw two stick figures on the board to represent the speakers in the dialog. You can also show that two people are speaking by changing your position or by shifting your weight from one foot to the other as you say each speaker's lines.

4. *Full-Class Choral Repetition*. Model each line and have the whole class repeat in unison.

5. Have students open their books and look at the dialog. Ask if there are any questions, and check understanding of new vocabulary.

6. *Group Choral Repetition*. Divide the class in half. Model line A and have Group 1 repeat. Model line B and have Group 2 repeat. Continue with all the lines of the model.

7. *Choral Conversation*. Have both groups practice the dialog twice, without a teacher model. First Group 1 is Speaker A and Group 2 is Speaker B; then reverse.

8. Call on one or two pairs of students to present the dialog.

In steps 6, 7, and 8, encourage students to look up from their books and *say* the lines rather than read them. (Students can of course refer to their books when necessary.)

The goal is not memorization or complete mastery of the model. Rather, students should become familiar with the model and feel comfortable saying it.

At this point, if you feel that additional practice is necessary before going on to the exercises, you can do Choral Conversation in small groups or by rows.

Alternative Approaches

Depending upon the abilities of your students and the particular lesson you're teaching, you might wish to try the following approaches to vary the way in which you introduce model conversations.

Pair Introduction

Have a pair of students present the model. Then practice it with the class.

Trio Introduction

Call on *three* students to introduce the model. Have two of them present it while the third acts as the *director*, offering suggestions for how to say the lines better. Then practice the dialog with the class.

Cloze Introduction

Write a cloze version of the model conversation on the board for student reference as you introduce the model. For lessons that provide a skeletal framework of the model (for example, Book 1 pp. 36, 64, 65, 101, 123), you can use that as the cloze version. For other lessons, you can decide which words to delete from the dialog.

Scrambled Dialog Introduction

Write each line of the dialog on a separate card. Distribute the cards to students. Have them practice saying their lines and then talk with each other to figure out what the correct order of the lines should be. Have them present the dialog to the class, each student in turn reading his or her line. Have the class decide if the dialog lines are in the correct order. Then practice the dialog with the class.

Warning: Do a scrambled dialog introduction *only* for conversations in which there is only one possible sentence order!

Disappearing Dialog Introduction

Write the dialog on the board and have students practice saying it. Erase a few of the words and practice again. Continue practicing the dialog several times, each time having erased more of the words, until the dialog has completely *disappeared* and students can say the lines without looking at them.

Eliciting the Model

Have students cover up the lines of the model and look just at the illustration. Ask questions based on the illustration and the situation. For example: *Who are these people? Where are they? What are they saying to each other?* As a class, in groups, or in pairs, have students suggest a possible dialog. Have students present their ideas and then compare them with the model conversation in the book. Then practice the dialog with the class.

Reviewing Model Conversations

Here are some possible ways to review model conversations from previous lessons.

Clap and Listen

Leave out words from the dialog while clapping your hands for the missing items. Students listen and fill in the missing words.

Sample Review Activity for Side by Side 1 page 42

a. With students' books closed, read the model conversation.
b. Read it again, this time clapping your hands or tapping on the desk to indicate missing words. For example: "[clap] is he?" Have students respond, "Who."
c. Read, "He's [clap] father." Have students respond "my."
d. Continue in the same way with the other lines of the conversation.

Different Emotions

> **Students present the model conversation using different emotions.**

Sample Review Activity for Side by Side 2 page 90

Have students practice reading the model conversation, using any combination of these different emotions:

> Speaker A is upset that she can't help her friend.
> Speaker A isn't upset that she can't help her friend.
> Speaker B is disappointed.
> Speaker B isn't disappointed.

Scrambled Dialogs

> **Write the lines from two or more model dialogs on separate cards and have students put them in the correct order.**

Sample Review Activity for Side by Side 3 pages 62 and 64

a. Write each line of the three model conversations from pages 62 and 64 on a separate card. Scramble the cards.
b. Give the cards to eight students. Have them unscramble the lines and put together the three conversations.
c. Form pairs and have each pair read a conversation.

VARIATION

a. Divide the class into three groups.
b. Make three sets of the model conversations from pages 62 and 64, writing each line on a separate card.
c. Give each group one set of the cards, and have the group members reorder the conversations.
d. Have each group read one of the conversations aloud while the others listen to check for accuracy.

Disappearing Dialogs

> **Students practice reading the model conversation several times, each time seeing fewer and fewer of the words.**

Sample Review Activity for Side by Side 4 page 134

a. Write the model conversation on the board.

b. Ask for two student volunteers to read the conversation.

c. Erase a few of the words from each line of the dialog. Have two different students read the conversation.

d. Erase more words and call on two more students to read the conversation.

e. Continue erasing words and calling on pairs of students to say the model until all the words have been erased and the dialog has *disappeared*.

Side by Side Exercises

The numbered exercises that follow the model form the core learning activity in each conversation lesson. Here students use the pictures and word cues to create conversations based on the structure of the model. Since all language practice in these lessons is conversational, you will always call on a pair of students to do each exercise. Your primary role is to serve as a resource to the class—to help students with new structures, new vocabulary, intonation, and pronunciation.

The *Teacher's Guides* recommend the following three steps for practicing the exercises. (Students should be given thorough practice with the first two exercises before going on.)

1. Exercise 1: Introduce any new vocabulary in the exercise. Call on two students to present the dialog. Then do Choral Repetition and Choral Conversation Practice.

2. Exercise 2: Same as for Exercise 1.

3. For the remaining exercises, there are two options: either Full-Class Practice or Pair Practice.

   Full-Class Practice: Call on a pair of students to do each exercise. Introduce new vocabulary one exercise at a time. (For more practice, you can call on other pairs of students or do Choral Repetition or Choral Conversation Practice.)

   Pair Practice: Introduce new vocabulary for all the exercises. Next have students practice all the exercises in pairs. Then have pairs present the exercises to the class. (For more practice, you can do Choral Repetition or Choral Conversation Practice.)

   The choice of Full-Class Practice or Pair Practice should be determined by the content of the particular lesson, the size and composition of the class, and your own teaching style. You might also wish to vary your approach from lesson to lesson.

Suggestions for Pairing Up Students

Whether you use Full-Class Practice or Pair Practice, you can select students for pairing in various ways.

- You might want to pair students by ability, since students of similar ability might work more efficiently together than students of dissimilar ability.

- On the other hand, you might wish to pair a weaker student with a stronger one. The slower student benefits from this pairing, while the more advanced student strengthens his or her abilities by helping a partner.

You should also encourage students to look at each other when speaking. This makes the conversational nature of the langauge practice more realistic. One way of ensuring this is *not* to call on two students who are sitting next to each other. Rather, call on students in different parts of the room and encourage them to look at each other when saying their lines.

Presenting New Vocabulary

Many new words are introduced in each conversation lesson. The illustration usually helps to convey the meaning, and the new words are written for students to see and use in these conversations. In addition, you might:

- write the new word on the board or on a word card
- say the new word several times and ask students to repeat chorally and individually
- help clarify the meaning with visuals.

Students might also find it useful to keep a notebook in which they write each new word, its meaning, and a sentence using that word.

Open-Ended Exercises

In many lessons, the final exercise is an open-ended one. This is indicated in the text by a blank box. Here students are expected to create conversations based on the structure of the model, but with vocabulary that they select themselves. This provides students with an opportunity for creativity, while still focusing on the particular structure being practiced. These open-ended exercises can be done orally in class and/or assigned as homework for presentation in class the next day. Encourage students to use dictionaries to find new words they want to use.

General Guiding Principles for Working with Guided Conversations

Speak, not *Read,* the Conversations

When doing the exercises, students should practice *speaking* to each other, rather than reading to each other. Even though students will need to refer to the text to be able to practice the conversations, they should not read the lines word by word. Rather, they should scan a full line and then look up from the book and *speak* the line to the other person.

Intonation and Gesture

Throughout, you should use the book to teach proper intonation and gesture. (Capitalized words are used to indicate spoken emphasis.) Students should be encouraged to truly *act out* the dialogs in a strong and confident voice.

Student-Centered Practice

Use of the texts should be as student-centered as possible. Modeling by the teacher should be efficient and economical, but students should have every opportunity to model for each other when they are capable of doing so.

Vocabulary in Context

Vocabulary can and should be effectively taught in the context of the conversation being practiced. Very often it will be possible to grasp the meaning from the conversation or its accompanying illustration. You should spend time drilling vocabulary in isolation only if you feel it is absolutely essential.

No "Grammar Talk"

Students need not study formally or be able to produce grammatical rules. The purpose of the texts is to engage students in active communication that gets them to *use* the language according to these rules.

Relating Lesson Content to Students' Lives and Experiences

Personalize the Exercises

While doing the guided conversation exercises, whenever you think it is appropriate, ask students questions that relate the situations in the exercises to their own lives and personal experiences. This will help make the leap from practicing language in the textbook to using the language for actual communication. For example:

For Side by Side 1 page 92

The focus of the lesson is the verb *have*. As students are presenting the exercises, ask them about things THEY have. For example:

> *Model Conversation*
> How about you? Do you have quiet neighbors or noisy neighbors?

> *Exercise 1*
> How about you? Do you have a cat or a dog? What's your cat's/dog's name?

> *Exercise 4*
> How about you? Do you have a brother or a sister? What's your brother's/sister's name?

For Side by Side 2 pages 46 and 47

The focus of the lesson is superlative adjectives. As students are presenting the exercises, ask them about people THEY know, using those superlative adjectives. For example:

> *Page 46, Exercise 1*
> Who is the friendliest person YOU know?
> In what ways is this person friendly?

> *Page 46, Exercise 9*
> Who is the sloppiest person YOU know?
> In what ways is this person sloppy?

> *Page 47, Exercise 5*
> Who is the most talented person YOU know?
> What things can this person do?

> *Page 47, Exercise 9*
> Who is the most generous person YOU know?
> In what ways is this person generous?

Interview the Characters

Where appropriate, as students are presenting the exercises to the class, as a way of making the situations come alive and making students feel as though they really *are* the characters in those situations, ask questions that students can respond to based on their imaginations. For example:

For Side by Side 2 pages 49-50

Before pairs of students present each of the exercises, ask the salesperson in each conversation the name of his or her store. Students can either use the name of a real store in their community or invent the name of a store where that particular product might be sold.

For Side by Side 3 pages 80-81

As a follow-up after each pair has presented its conversation involving an important decision someone has made, interview that person and ask what the reasons were for making that decision.

Options for Additional Practice

These activities are appropriate as follow-ups after students have practiced the model conversation and exercises in the lesson.

Who Is It?

Make statements about characters in the exercises and have students guess which person you're talking about.

Note: This activity is appropriate *only* for exercises in which characters are named.

For Side by Side 1 page 110

Make statements about the people in the exercises. Have students respond by telling who you're talking about. For example:

This person has a toothache.	Nancy	*(Exercise 3)*
These people are studying.	Carl and Tim	*(Exercise 5)*
This person needs money.	Ted	*(Exercise 7)*
This person has dirty laundry.	Linda	*(Exercise 6)*
These people need food.	George and Martha	*(Exercise 2)*
This person is in the garage.	Peggy	*(Exercise 1)*
This person is sick.	Michael	*(Model Conversation)*
This person's living room is dirty.	Henry	*(Exercise 4)*

Guided Conversation Match Game

Students match sentences with their appropriate rejoinders.

Note: This activity is appropriate *only* as a review for lessons in which the conversations consist of two-line exchanges.

Sample Review Activity for Side by Side 1 page 147

a. Make a set of cards with Speaker A's and Speaker B's lines from the following conversations:

Did you sleep well last night?	Yes, I did. I was tired.
Did Roger sleep well last night?	No, he didn't. He wasn't tired.

Did Tom have a big breakfast today?	Yes, he did. He was hungry.
Did Jane have a big breakfast today?	No, she didn't. She wasn't hungry.
Did Mrs. Brown go to the doctor yesterday?	Yes, she did. She was sick.
Did Mr. Brown go to the doctor yesterday?	No, he didn't. He wasn't sick.
Did Timothy finish his milk?	Yes, he did. He was thirsty.
Did Jennifer finish her milk?	No, she didn't. She wasn't thirsty.
Did Susan miss the train?	Yes, she did. She was late.

b. Distribute the cards to students.

c. Have students memorize the phrase on their cards and then walk around the room, saying their phrase until they find their match.

d. Then have pairs of students say their matched sentences aloud to the class.

Tell More About It

Students invent additional information about a situation in the text.

Sample Review Activity for Side by Side 3 page 3

Have students look at the illustration for Exercise 6 (a young girl writing a letter to her grandparents) and ask the following questions:

> What's Mary doing?
> Does she write to her grandparents often?
> What does she write to them about?

Does she see them often?

What does Mary do with her grandparents when she sees them?

Have students use their imaginations to tell more about Mary.

Continue the Conversation

Students create role plays in which a conversation continues.

Sample Review Activity for Side by Side 1 pages 122-123

a. Divide the class into pairs.

b. Have each pair choose one of the conversations in the lesson—either the model or any of the exercises—and create a role play in which that conversation continues.

c. Have the pairs present their role plays to the class and compare their continuations of the situation.

Surprise Situations

Students are presented with a new situation and must create a conversation using that *surprise* information.

VARIATION 1: USING A SKELETAL FRAMEWORK

Sample Review Activity for Side by Side 3 pages 66-67

a. Put a skeletal framework of the model conversation on the board:

> A. You look tired. What _____ doing?
>
> B. I've been _____ since _____.
>
> A. Really? How many _____?
>
> B. Believe it or not, _____ already _____.
>
> A. _____?! No wonder you're tired!

b. Ask for a pair of student volunteers to come to the front of the room.

c. Give them word cards such as the following and have them create a conversation based on the framework on the board, using the information on their cards. They should feel free to modify the conversation any way they wish.

Speaker A:	Speaker B:
Your friend looks tired.	You've been making cookies since _____.

Other possible pairs of cards:

Speaker A:	Speaker B:
Your friend looks tired.	You've been doing grammar exercises since _____.

Speaker A:	Speaker B:
Your friend looks tired.	You've been filling out job applications since _____.

VARIATION 2: USING KEY WORDS

Sample Activity for Side by Side 3 pages 68-69

a. Write key words from the model conversation on the board:

> A. nervous
> B. Why?
> A. going to
>   never/before
> B. Don't worry!
>   for years
>   Believe me!

b. Ask for a pair of student volunteers to come to the front of the room.

c. Give them word cards such as the following and have them create a conversation based on the model conversation from the text, using the key words on the board and the information on their cards. They should feel free to modify the conversation any way they wish.

Speaker A:	Speaker B:
You're nervous!	Your friend is nervous.
You're going to go skydiving!	Give your friend some encouragement.

Other possible pairs of cards:

Speaker A:	Speaker B:
Your friend is nervous.	Your friend is nervous.
Your going to sing in a karaoke club!	Give your friend some encouragement.

Speaker A:	Speaker B:
You're nervous!	Your friend is nervous.
You're going to climb Mt. Fuji!	Give your friend some encouragement.

We encourage you to try some of these approaches as well as the communication activities that follow. In keeping with the spirit of *Side by Side*, they are intended to provide students with a language learning experience that is dynamic ... interactive ... and fun!

Steven J. Molinsky
Bill Bliss

Side by Side Communication Activities

1. Ask Me a Question!

Students ask each other questions to guess a *mystery* person, place, thing, or action.

Sample Activity for Side by Side 2 pages 49–50

a. Divide the class into groups of three or four.

b. One student in each group thinks of something you can buy at a department store.

c. The other students in the group then try to guess the item by asking yes/no questions. For example:

> *[thinking of a rocking chair]*
>
> Student 1: I'm thinking of something you can buy at a department store.
>
> Student 2: Do you wear it?
> Student 1: No, you don't.
>
> Student 3: Do you listen to it?
> Student 1: No, you don't.
>
> Student 4: Do you sit on it?
> Student 1: Yes, you do.
>
> Student 2: Is it comfortable?
> Student 1: Yes, it is.
>
> Student 3: Is it a sofa?
> Student 1: No, it isn't.
>
> Student 4: Is it a rocking chair?
> Student 1: Yes, it is.

d. Have the remaining students in each group take their turn thinking of something for the others to guess.

2. Associations

Sample Activity for Side by Side 1 page 107

a. Divide the class into pairs or small groups.

b. Call out the name of an occupation and tell students to write down all the words they associate with that occupation. For example:

mechanic: car, fix, garage
chef: cook, restaurant, food
violinist: music, play, songs

c. Have a student from each pair or group come to the board and write their words.

Option: Do the activity as a game, in which you divide the class into teams. The team with the most associations is the winner.

3. Beanbag Toss

Students call out vocabulary items while tossing a beanbag to each other.

Sample Activity for Side by Side 1 page 64

Have students toss a beanbag back and forth. The student to whom the beanbag is tossed names a color. For example:

Student 1: red
Student 2: green
Student 3: purple
etc.

Students call out short sentences while tossing a beanbag to each other.

Sample Activity for Side by Side 1 pages 25–26

Have students toss a beanbag back and forth. The student to whom the beanbag is tossed says an activity. For example:

Student 1: I'm washing my hair.
Student 2: I'm cleaning my yard.
Student 3: I'm doing my exercises.
etc.

4. Bleep!

Sample Activity for Side by Side 2 page 18

a. Write the following vocabulary words on cards, mix up the cards, and put them face down in a pile on a table or desk in front of the room:

can	jar	bottle	box
bag	loaf	bunch	head
pound	quart	dozen	

b. Divide the class into pairs.

c. Have each pair come to the front of the room, pick two cards from the pile, and create a conversation in which they use those two words.

d. Call on the pairs to present their conversations to the class. However, instead of saying the two words when they come up in the conversations, students should say the word *bleep* instead!

e. Other students then try to guess the *bleeped* words. For example:

    A. Do we need anything at the supermarket?
    B. Yes. We need a *bleep* of flour.
    A. Do we need anything else?
    B. Yes. We also need two *bleeps* of vegetable soup.

5. Board Game

Students play a board game in which they answer questions.

Sample Activity for Side by Side 1 pages 32–33

a. On poster boards or on manila file folders, make up game boards with a pathway consisting of separate spaces. You may use any theme or design you wish.

b. Divide the class into groups of two to four students and give each group a game board, a die, and something to be used as a playing piece.

c. Give each group a pile of cards face-down with questions such as the following:

> What's the opposite of <u>young</u>?
> What's the opposite of <u>heavy</u>?

d. Each student in turn rolls the die, moves the playing piece along the game path, and after landing on a space, picks a card and answers the question.

Option: You should decide on the rules of the game. You may want each student to take his or her turn only once, or you may want a student who successfully answers a question to take another turn.

e. The first student to reach the end of the pathway is the winner.

Sample Activity for Side by Side 1 page 73

a. On poster boards or on manila file folders, make up game boards with a pathway consisting of separate spaces. You may use any theme or design you wish.

b. Divide the class into groups of two to four students and give each group a game board, a die, and something to be used as a playing piece.

c. Give each group a pile of cards face-down with sentences written on them. Some sentences should be correct, and others incorrect. For example:

> She lives in Hong Kong.
> He read the newspaper every day.
> I listens to Italian music.
> They drink English tea.
> We speaks Japanese.

d. Each student in turn rolls the die, moves the playing piece along the game path, and after landing on a space, picks a card, reads the sentence, and says if it is *correct* or *incorrect*. If the sentence is incorrect and the student is able to give the correct version, that student takes an additional turn.

e. The first student to reach the end of the pathway is the winner.

6. Build Your Vocabulary!

Students keep a record of new words they encounter outside of class.

This activity is appropriate for any Side by Side lesson.

Have students carry a small notebook with them as they go about their daily lives. Encourage them to write down new phrases or words they hear. At the beginning of each class, have one student volunteer to tell the class his or her new vocabulary words and expressions and the contexts in which they were found. Have the rest of the class try to guess the meaning of the words and expressions.

7. Can You Hear the Difference?

Students discriminate between similar sounding words or sentences.

Sample Activity for Side by Side 2 page 31

a. Write on the board:

Present	Future
I go swimming.	I'll go swimming.
You go swimming.	You'll go swimming.
We go swimming.	We'll go swimming.
They go swimming.	They'll go swimming.

b. Choose a sentence randomly from one of the two columns and say it to the class. Have the class listen and identify whether the sentence is in the present or in the future.

c. Have students continue the activity in pairs. One student pronounces a sentence and the other identifies the tense. Then have them reverse roles.

d. Write other similar sentences on the board and continue the practice.

8. Category Dictation

Establish columns for different vocabulary or grammatical categories. Dictate words and have students write them under the appropriate category.

Sample Activity for Side by Side 2 page 12

a. Have students draw two columns on a piece of paper. At the top of one column, have students write <u>Things I eat</u>, and at the top of the other column, have them write <u>Things I drink</u>.

b. Dictate various food items from the text and have students write them in the appropriate column. For example:

<u>Things I eat</u>	<u>Things I drink</u>
ice cream	coffee
rice	milk
cookies	soda

Sample Activity for Side by Side 1 pages 100–101

a. Have students draw two columns on a piece of paper. At the top of one column, have students write <u>right now</u>, and at the top of the other column, have them write <u>every day</u>.

b. Dictate verb phrases and have students write them in the appropriate column. For example:

<u>right now</u>	<u>every day</u>
I'm cooking	I cook
we're sleeping	we sleep
she's studying	she studies

9. Chain Game

Students extend a sentence by adding more and more vocabulary items.

Sample Activity for Side by Side 1 page 64

a. Begin the game by saying:

> "I'm looking for a (green jacket)."
> (You can name any color and clothing item you wish.)

b. Have each student take a turn in which he or she repeats what the person before said and adds a new color and clothing item. For example:

> "I'm looking for a green jacket and a black belt."
> "I'm looking for a green jacket, a black belt, and a striped blouse."

Sample Activity for Side by Side 1 page 137

a. Begin the game by saying:

> "I had a busy day today. I went to the bank."

b. Have each student take a turn in which he or she repeats what the person before said and adds a new activity. For example:

> "I had a busy day today. I went to the bank, and I read a book."
> "I had a busy day today. I went to the bank, I read a book, and I wrote to my grandfather."

10. Chain Story

Students create a story by adding one new sentence at a time.

Sample Activity for Side by Side 2 pages 118–119

a. Begin by saying, "I couldn't fall asleep last night because all my neighbors were making noise."

b. Student 1 repeats what you said and adds another item. For example: "I couldn't fall asleep last night because all my neighbors were making noise. My downstairs neighbors were listening to loud music."

c. Continue around the room in this fashion, with each student repeating what the previous one said and adding another sentence.

d. You can do the activity again, beginning and ending with different students.

If the class is large, you may want to divide students into groups to give students more practice.

11. Change the Sentence!

Sample Activity for Side by Side 1 page 121

a. Write a sentence on the board, underlining and numbering different portions of the sentence. For example:

1	2	3
I'm going to	go to the bank	tomorrow.

b. Have students sit in a circle.

c. Tell them that when you say a number, the first student in the circle makes a change in that part of the sentence. For example:

Teacher: Two.
Student 1: I'm going to go swimming tomorrow.

d. The second student keeps the first student's sentence, but changes it based on the next number you say. For example:

Teacher: Three.
Student 2: I'm going to go swimming this week.

e. Continue this way with the rest of the students in the circle. For example:

Teacher: One.
Student 3: He's going to go swimming this week.

Teacher: Two.
Student 4: He's going to see a movie this week.

12. Clap in Rhythm

Sample Activity for Side by Side 1 page 51

a. Have students sit in a circle.

b. Establish a steady, even beat (one-two-three-four, one-two-three-four) by having students clap their hands to their laps twice and then clap their hands together twice. Repeat throughout the game, maintaining the same rhythm.

c. The object is for each student in turn to name a place around town each time the hands are clapped together twice. Nothing is said when students clap their hands on their laps.

Note: The beat never stops! If a student misses a beat, he or she can either wait for the next beat or else pass to the next student.

13. Class Discussion

Students discuss situations presented in the text.

Sample Activity for Side by Side 3 pages 31–32

a. Write the following questions on the board or on a handout for students:

> Do your friends or neighbors ever ask you to do a favor for them?
> How do you feel when someone asks you to do a favor?
> What was the biggest favor someone asked you to do? Tell about it.

b. Divide the class into small groups and have students discuss doing favors. Then call on students to tell about their discussions.

14. Class Story

Students develop a story based on a situation from the text.

Sample Activity for Side by Side 2 pages 80–81

a. Have students look at one of the illustrations on page 80 or 81 of the text.

b. Ask questions about one of the situations to help them imagine a storyline. For example (using Exercise 4 on page 81):

> What are these people's names
> What happened to them?
> How did they feel?
> What did they do next?
> Then what happened?

c. Have students dictate the story to you as you write it on the board. Ask them how to spell various words as they're dictating the story to you. Also, ask the class to point out any grammar errors they find in the story.

15. Concentration

Sample Activity for Side by Side 1 page 73

a. Write 12 sentences based on the people in the exercises on pages 72 or 73. For example:

He lives in Rome.	He speaks Italian.
She lives in Athens.	She speaks Greek.
He lives in Tokyo.	He speaks Japanese.

b. Shuffle the cards and place them face down in three rows of four each.

c. Divide the class into two teams. The object of the game is for students to find the matching cards. Both teams should be able to see all the cards, since *concentrating* on their location is an important part of playing the game.

d. A student from Team 1 turns over two cards. If they match, the student picks up the cards, that team gets a point, and the student takes another turn. If the cards don't match, the student turns them face down, and a member of Team 2 takes a turn.

e. The game continues until all the cards have been matched. The team with the most correct matches wins the game.

Option: This game can also be played in groups and pairs.

Sample Activity for Side by Side 4 pages 120–121

a. Write the following sentences on separate cards:

I got a raise!	You did?
I'm going to move to Miami.	You are?
I've been fired!	You have?
I was robbed last night!	You were?

I'll probably sell my car.	You will?
I meditate every day.	You do?

b. Shuffle the cards and place them face down in three rows of four each.

c. Divide the class into two teams. The object of the game is for students to find the matching cards. Both teams should be able to see all the cards, since *concentrating* on their location is an important part of playing the game.

d. A student from Team 1 turns over two cards. If they match, the student picks up the cards, that team gets a point, and the student takes another turn. If the cards don't match, the student turns them face down, and a member of Team 2 takes a turn.

e. The game continues until all the cards have been matched. The team with the most correct matches wins the game.

Option: This game can also be played in groups and pairs.

16. Conversation Framework

Sample Activity for Side by Side 2 page 21

Have students use a conversational model to talk about their favorite places to eat, such as restaurants or coffee shops.

a. Write on the board:

> A. Where do you like to eat?
>
> B. I like to eat at _____.
>
> A. Oh, really? What do you recommend?
>
> B. I recommend the _____. (It's/They're) _____.
>   How about you? Where do you like to eat?
>
> A. I like to eat at _____. The _____ there
>   (is/are) _____.

b. Have pairs of students create conversations. Encourage students to expand the dialog in any way they wish.

Example:

> A. Where do you like to eat?
> B. I like to eat at Stanley's Restaurant.
> A. Oh, really? What do you recommend?
> B. I recommend the chicken. It's excellent.
>   How about you? Where do you like to eat?
> A. I like to eat at Mr. Burger. The hamburgers there are fantastic.

17. Correct the Statement!

Sample Activity for Side by Side 1 page 64

Make statements about students in the class. Some statements should be true, and others false. Have students repond to your statements. If a statement is false, a student should correct it. For example:

> Teacher: Michael is wearing black shoes today.
> Student: That's right.

> Teacher: Carla is wearing a red blouse.
> Student: No, she isn't. She's wearing a white skirt.

Option 1: Have students make statements for others to react to.

Option 2: Do the activity as a game with two competing teams.

Sample Activity for Side by Side 1 page 91

a. Write on the board:

| always | usually | sometimes | rarely | never |

b. Call on students to make statements about others in the class, using one of the words on the board.

c. Have people respond "That's true" or "That's not true" after each statement is made. If someone responds "That's not true," then he or she must correct the statement. For example:

> A. Maria usually comes to class on time.
> B. That's true.

> A. Robert rarely does his English homework.
> B. That's not true. He always does his English homework.

18. Describe the Picture!

Students describe pictures designed to elicit specific vocabulary or grammar structures.

Sample Activity for Side by Side 1 page 65

Bring in pictures that depict clothing items from magazines, newspapers, or mail order clothing catalogs. As a class, in pairs, or in small groups, have students describe what the people in the pictures are wearing.

19. Dialog Builder!

Give students a line from a dialog and have them create a conversation incorporating that line.

Sample Activity for Side by Side 2 page 31

a. Divide the class into pairs.

b. Write a line on the board from a conversation such as the following:

| I'm afraid I might get sick. |

Other possible lines:

> I'm afraid I'll have a terrible time.
> I'm afraid I might get hurt.
> I'm afraid I might fall.
> I'm sure I'll fall asleep.

c. Have each pair create a conversation incorporating that line. Students can begin and end their conversations any way they wish, but they must include that line in their dialogs.

d. Call on students to present their conversations to the class.

20. Dictate and Discuss

Dictate sentences and have students discuss them.

Sample Activity for Side by Side 2 pages 39–40

    a. Divide the class into pairs or small groups.

    b. Dictate sentences such as the following and then have students discuss them:

> Dogs are friendlier than cats.
>
> Used cars are better than new cars.
>
> English is easier than ____*(other language)*____ .
>
> Our city is more beautiful than _____*(other city)*_____ .

    c. Call on students to share their opinions with the rest of the class.

21. Dictation Game

Pairs of students dictate sentences to each other.

Sample Activity for Side by Side 2 page 60

    a. Make up a four- to five-sentence set of directions. Write the directions in large print on a piece of paper. For example:

> Take the Main Street bus.
> Get off at First Avenue.
> Walk down First Avenue to River Street.
> Turn right.
> You'll see the zoo on the left.

    b. Put the paper on the far side of the room or out in the hallway so that students can't read it from their seats.

    c. Divide the class into pairs. One student from each pair runs to read the directions and then returns to dictate the directions to the partner. The runner may go back and forth as many times as necessary. The first pair to finish the set of directions wins.

22. Do You Remember?

Students try to remember what they saw in a picture.

Sample Activity for Side by Side 1 page 27

VARIATION 1: SPEAKING ACTIVITY

   a. Tell students to spend three minutes looking carefully at the illustration on page 27.

   b. Have students close their books.

   c. Ask questions to see how much they remember about the scene. For example:

> Where are Mr. and Mrs. Sharp?
> What are they doing?
>
> Where is Patty Williams?
> What's she doing?

Option: Divide the class into teams and do the activity as a game. The team with the most correct answers wins.

VARIATION 2: WRITING ACTIVITY

   a. Divide the class into pairs.

   b. Tell students to spend three minutes looking carefully at the illustration on page 27.

   c. Have students close their books and write down what they remember about the scene.

   d. Have students compare their sentences with their partner and then look at the illustration in the book to see how much they remembered.

Note: This activity can also be done with any picture you bring to class from a newspaper or magazine depicting situations relevant to a particular *Side by Side* lesson.

23. Draw, Write, and Read

Students draw and write descriptions.

Sample Activity for Side by Side 1 page 54

   a. Have students draw a picture of their house or apartment. Also, have them write a description to accompany the picture.

   b. In pairs, have students describe their homes as they show their pictures.

24. Drawing Game

Students draw vocabulary words for others to guess.

Sample Activity for Side by Side 2 page 18

a. Write down on two sets of cards as many of the following food vocabulary items as you wish:

bananas	bread	carrots	milk
onions	cheese	soda	oranges
lettuce	apples	butter	eggs
tomatoes	lemons	french fries	ice cream
rice	meatballs	cake	cookies
grapes			

b. Divide the class into two teams. Have each team sit together in a different part of the room.

c. Place each set of cards on a table or desk in front of the room. Also place a pad of paper and pencil next to each team's set of cards.

d. When you say, "Go!", a person from each team comes to the table, picks a card from that team's pile, draws the item on the card, and shows the drawing to the rest of the team. The team then guesses what the word is.

e. When a team correctly guesses a word, another team member picks a card and draws the word written on that card.

f. Continue until each team has guessed all the words in their pile.

g. The team that guesses the words in the shortest time wins the game.

25. Expand the Sentence!

> **Students take turns adding words to expand a sentence.**

Sample Activity for Side by Side 3 pages 7–8

Tell students that the object of the activity is to build a long sentence on the board, one word at a time.

a. Call on a student to write a pronoun or someone's name on the far left side of the board. For example:

> George

b. Have another student come to the board and add a word. For example:

> George likes

c. Have a third student add a third word. For example:

> George likes to

d. Continue until each student in the class has had one or more turns to add a word to expand the sentence into the longest one they can think of. For example:

> George likes to talk to his brother on the telephone every Sunday night because his brother lives in Russia and George doesn't talk to his brother very often.

26. Find the Right Person!

> **Students have information about others in the class and interview each other to identify the correct people.**

VARIATION 1: USING A MASTER GRID

Sample Activity for Side by Side 1 page 92

a. Collect some information about what students *have*.

b. Put the information in the following form:

```
Find someone who . . .

1. has a new computer.      _____

2. has a large dog.         _____

3. has noisy neighbors.     _____

4. has three sisters.       _____

5. has a guitar.            _____
```

c. Have students circulate around the room, asking each other questions to identify the above people. For example:

> Do you have a new computer?
> Do you have a large dog?

d. The first student to find all the people, raise his or her hand, and tell the class who the people are is the winner of the game. For example:

> Alice has a new computer.   Barbara has three sisters.
> Miguel has a large dog.   Roberto has a guitar.
> Peter has noisy neighbors.

VARIATION 2: USING STUDENTS' STATEMENTS

Sample Activity for Side by Side 3 page 74

a. Write the following on the board:

```
I like to _____.

I enjoy _____ ing.

_____ ing is my favorite way to relax.
```

b. Have students then complete these sentences on a separate piece of paper with real information about themselves.

c. Collect the papers and distribute them randomly to everyone in the class.

d. Have students interview each other in order to find the correct person to match the information they have. For example:

> Do you like to *(ski)*?
> Do you enjoy *(going to movies)*?
> Is *(reading)* your favorite way to relax?

e. Have students report back to the class.

Option: This activity can be done as a game, in which the first student to identify the correct person is the winner.

27. Finish the Sentence!

Students complete sentences with appropriate vocabulary words.

Variation 1: Sentence Completion

Sample Activity for Side by Side 1 pages 25–26

Begin a sentence and have students repeat what you said and add appropriate endings to the sentence. For example:

Teacher	Students
I'm washing . . .	I'm washing my car.
	I'm washing my windows.
	I'm washing my clothes.
He's feeding . . .	He's feeding his dog.
	He's feeding his cat.
We're cleaning . . .	We're cleaning our yard.
	We're cleaning our apartment.
	We're cleaning our garage.
She's doing . . .	She's doing her homework.
	She's doing her exercises.
They're painting . . .	They're painting their kitchen.
	They're painting their bedroom.
	They're painting their bathroom.

Option: This activity may be done as a class, in pairs or small groups, or as a game with competing teams.

Variation 2: Word Cues on the Board

Sample Activity for Side by Side 3 page 13

a. Write the following words on the board:

angry	hungry	on time	scared	tired
bored	nervous	prepared	thirsty	upset

b. Read the following incomplete sentences and have students complete each with the appropriate word from the board:

He drank two bottles of soda because he was very . . .
I didn't know the answers on the test because I wasn't . . .
Kathy didn't want to go to into that dark room because she was . . .
Bob fell asleep in class because he was . . .
I didn't have any lunch today, and now I'm . . .

Class began at nine. I arrived at nine thirty. I wasn't . . .
My little brother cried because he was . . .
Your big exam is tomorrow. Are you feeling . . . ?
Paul had an accident with his father's car. His father was very . . .
It rained all day yesterday. I stayed home and didn't do anything. I was . . .

Option: Divide the class into teams and do the activity as a game. Say a sentence, and the first person to raise his or her hand and complete the sentence correctly gets a point for that team. The team with the most points wins the game.

28. Finish the Sentence Line-Up

Students line up opposite each other and complete sentences.

Sample Activity for Side by Side 3 page 104

a. Write the following two-word verbs on the board:

put away	call up	turn on
hang up	take back	throw out
pick up	pick out	fill out

b. Have students line up in two rows opposite each other.

c. Have the first student in the *left* row begin a sentence with one of the verbs on the board. The opposite student in the *right* row must complete the sentence. For example:

Student 1: I turned on . . .
Student 2: the heat.

d. Then have the next student in the *right* row begin a sentence with another verb, and the opposite student in the *left* row complete it. For example:

Student 3: He hung up . . .
Student 4: the picture.

e. Continue going back and forth until all the students have had an opportunity to either begin or complete a sentence.

29. Grammar Chain

Students do a chain game exercise with a grammatical focus.

Sample Activity for Side by Side 1 page 137

a. Start the chain game by saying:

> Teacher: I went skiing yesterday.
> (*to Student A*) Did *you* go skiing yesterday?

b. Student A must answer, "No, I didn't," make a new statement using the verb *go*, and ask Student B, who then continues the chain. For example:

> Student A: No, I didn't. I went skating.
> (*to Student B*) Did *you* go skating?

> Student B: No, I didn't. I went bowling.
> (*to Student C*) Did *you* go bowling?
> etc.

30. Group Story

Groups of students create stories which they retell to the class.

Sample Activity for Side by Side 2 pages 118–119

a. Write on the board:

> Yesterday was one of the worst days _____ can remember!

b. Divide the class into small groups of three to five students.

c. Have each group create a story of at least ten sentences about a person who had a very bad day yesterday. Encourage students to use any vocabulary they wish and to draw from their own experiences in describing the unlucky events.

d. Have one person from each group present that group's story to the class.

e. Have the class decide which group's story describes the worst day of all.

31. Guess the Word!

Students try to guess a word by asking yes/no questions.

Sample Activity for Side by Side 2 pages 58–59

a. Tell each student to think of a place around town.

b. Have a student come to the front of the room and say, "I'm thinking of a place around town."

c. The other students try to guess the place by asking yes/no questions. For example:

> Do you buy food there?
> Do you watch the animals there?
> Do you wash your clothes there?

32. How Many Questions?

Give students answers to questions and have them try to create as many questions for that answer as they can.

Sample Activity for Side by Side 4 pages 38–39

a. Divide the class into pairs or small groups.

b. Write an answer sentence on the board such as the following:

> You should ask the teacher.

c. Have students create as many questions as they can think of that might be answered by that statement. For example:

> Do you know if we're going to have a test this week?
> Do you by any chance know what tomorrow's homework assignment is?
> Can you tell me what this word means?
> Do you have any idea why English is so complicated?

d. The pair or group with the most correct sentences is the winner.

e. Continue the activity with additional answer sentences. For example:

> You should ask your doctor.
> You should ask your boss.
> You should ask that police officer.

33. How Many Sentences?

Students make up sentences based on a group of words.

Sample Activity for Side by Side 3 page 3

a. Write the following on the board:

bake	-s
cook	-ing
chicken	the
kitchen	is
clean	in
chef	are

b. Divide the class into pairs or small groups.

c. Tell students that the object of the game is to see how many sentences they can think of based on these words. Explain that *-ing* can be added to verbs (for example: *cooking, baking*), and *-s* can be added to verbs (*cooks, bakes*) and to nouns (*chickens, chefs*).

Decide if you'd prefer the activity to be oral or written. Students can say their sentences or they can write them.

Some possible sentences:

The chicken is cooking in the kitchen.
The chefs are cleaning chickens in the kitchen.
The chickens are clean.
Clean the kitchen!
The chef's kitchen is clean.
The chicken is baking in the kitchen.
The chef bakes chickens in the clean kitchen.

Option: You can do this activity as a game, in which the pair or group of students who comes up with the most sentences wins.

34. In Your Opinion

Students express their opinions based on content of the textbook lesson.

Sample Activity for Side by Side 2 pages 49-50

a. Divide the class into pairs or small groups.

b. Have the pairs or groups discuss the following:

> In your opinion, what's the best place in town to buy a good refrigerator?
> What's the best place to buy a comfortable rocking chair?
> What's the best place to buy a good tape recorder?
> What's the best place to buy a good, cheap watch?

c. Have students report back to the class. Make a list of students' suggestions and, if you wish, publish them as a class guide to shopping in the community.

Sample Activity for Side by Side 4 pages 24-25

a. Have students read a newspaper and come to the next class with answers to questions such as the following:

> In your opinion, what was the most important thing that happened in the world?
> Who was the most interesting person you read about?
> What was the funniest thing you read?

b. Have students compare their answers.

35. Information Gap Handouts

Pairs of students compare different information.

Sample Activity for Side by Side 2 pages 2–3

a. Tell students that your friend John is going to have a very busy week next week. He has a lot of things to do. Make up a schedule for John's week, but divide the information between two different schedules. For example:

Schedule A:

Sun.	Mon.	Tues.	Wed.	Thurs.	Fri.	Sat.
clean his house		plant flowers in his garden		wash the floors and vacuum the carpets		relax and watch TV

Schedule B:

Sun.	Mon.	Tues.	Wed.	Thurs.	Fri.	Sat.
	paint his fence		cook spaghetti and bake apple pies		fix his broken front steps	

b. Divide the class into pairs. Give each member of the pair a different schedule. Have students share their information and fill in their schedules. For example:

Student A: John is going to clean his house on Sunday.
Student B: Okay. *[writes the information in Schedule B]* On Monday he's going to paint his fence.

c. The pairs continue until each has a filled calendar.

d. Have students look at their partner's schedule to make sure that they have written the information correctly.

36. Information Gap Role Play

Students create role plays in which each student has different information.

Sample Activity for Side by Side 3 pages 31-32

a. Divide the class into pairs.

b. Write the following situations on index cards and give one of the situations to each pair. Give Role A to one member of the pair and Role B to the other.

c. Have students practice their role plays and then present them to the class. Compare different students' versions of the same situations.

Role A:

Your car is broken, and you need a ride to work today. Ask your friend.

Role B:

You aren't going to work today because you have a very bad cold.

Role A:

Your bicycle has a flat tire, and you can't find your jack. Ask your friend.

Role B:

Your sister borrowed your jack last week, and she forgot to return it.

Role A:

You're baking a cake, and you just realized that you don't have any more flour! Your next-door neighbor is walking out of the building. Maybe your neighbor is going to the supermarket.

Role B:

You're walking out of your apartment building. First, you're going to the bank. Then you're going to the post office. After that, you're going to the drug store. And finally, you're going to the supermarket.

37. Information Search

Students look for answers to questions and report back to the class.

Sample Activity for Side by Side 4 page 60

a. Have students look in the local newspaper to see what activities are taking place in their community over the weekend.

b. Have students report their findings to the class.

38. Interview

Students interview each other and report back to the class.

Sample Activity for Side by Side 1 page 117

a. Write the following on the board:

> What are you going to do this weekend?

b. Have pairs of students interview each other and then report back to the class about their partner's weekend plans.

39. Key Word Role Play

Students create role plays incorporating key words and structures from the lesson.

Sample Activity for Side by Side 3 pages 52-53

a. Write the following on the board:

> interested in?
> live?
> work?
> how long?

b. Divide the class into pairs.

c. Tell each pair that they've just met at a party. Have them create a role play, using the key expressions on the board.

d. Call on pairs to present their role plays to the class.

40. Letter Game

Students guess vocabulary items based on the first letter.

Sample Activity for Side by Side 1 pages 62-63

a. Divide the class into two teams.

b. Say, "I'm thinking of something you wear that starts with *c*."

c. The first person to raise his or her hand and guess correctly *[coat]* wins a point for his or her team.

d. Continue with other letters of the alphabet and clothing items.

The team that gets the most correct answers wins the game.

41. Match the Conversations

Students match sentences with their appropriate rejoinders.

Sample Activity for Side by Side 1 page 107

a. Make a set of matching cards based on occupations. For example:

Can you fix cars?	Of course I can. I'm a very good mechanic.
Can you sing?	Of course I can. I'm a very good singer.
Can you cook?	Of course I can. I'm a very good chef.
Can you act?	Of course I can. I'm a very good (actor/actress).
Can you play the violin?	Of course I can. I'm a very good violinist.
Can you drive a truck?	Of course I can. I'm a very good truck driver.
Can you dance?	Of course I can. I'm a very good dancer.
Can you teach?	Of course I can. I'm a very good teacher.
Can you bake pies?	Of course I can. I'm a very good baker.

b. Distribute a card to each student.

c. Have students memorize the phrase on their cards, and then have students walk around the room saying their phrase until they find their match.

d. Then have pairs of students say their matched sentences aloud to the class.

42. *Match the Sentences*

Students match beginnings of sentences with their corresponding conclusions.

Sample Activity for Side by Side 2 page 79

   a. Make a set of split sentence cards such as the following:

I went to the movies . . .	by myself.
My brother had a picnic . . .	by himself.
My sister went to the ballgame . . .	by herself.
My friend and I took a long walk . . .	by ourselves.
Our neighbors painted their house . . .	by themselves.
The car started . . .	by itself.
You can't fix that . . .	by yourself.

   b. Distribute a card to each student.

   c. Have students memorize the sentence portion on their cards and then walk around the room trying to find their corresponding match.

   d. Then have pairs of students say their completed sentences aloud to the class.

43. Memory Chain

Students try to remember what others have said.

Sample Activity for Side by Side 3 pages 68-69

a. Divide the class into groups of five or six students each.

b. Tell each student to think of something that he or she has never done.

c. One group at a time, have Student 1 begin. For example:

   I've never given blood.

d. Student 2 repeats what Student 1 said and adds a statement about himself or herself. For example:

   Marco has never given blood, and I've never run in a marathon.

e. Student 3 continues in the same way. For example:

   Marco has never given blood, Carol has never run in a marathon, and I've never ridden a motorcycle.

f. Continue until everyone has had a chance to play the *memory chain*.

44. Miming

Students pantomime, and others guess what they're pantomiming.

Sample Activity for Side by Side 1 pages 18-19

a. Write down on cards the activities from text pages 18 and 19.

b. Have students take turns picking a card from the pile and pantomiming the action on the card.

c. The class must guess what the person is doing.

Option: This can be done as a game with two competing teams.

45. Mystery Conversations

Students create conversations, and others guess the situation.

Sample Activity for Side by Side 3 page 41

a. Divide the class into pairs.

b. Write the following conversational framework on the board:

> Have you _____ ed yet?

c. Write roles such as the following on word cards and give one to each pair of students:

a parent and a child	a boss and an employee
a teacher and a student	two friends
two neighbors	a nurse and a patient
a wife and a husband	a brother and a sister

d. Have each pair create a short dialog that begins "Have you _____ ed yet?" The dialogs should be appropriate for the roles the students have on their cards.

e. Have each pair present their dialog to the class. Then have the other students guess who the people are: Are they friends? Is a teacher talking to a student? For example:

> *[parent–child]*
> A. Have you cleaned your room yet?
> B. No, I haven't. But I'm going to clean it tonight.
> A. Well, please don't forget. I've already asked you two times.
> B. Don't worry. I won't forget.

> *[boss–employee]*
> A. Have you typed those letters yet?
> B. Yes, I have. I just finished typing them a few minutes ago.
> A. Can I see them, please?
> B. Certainly. Here they are.

46. Mystery Word

Students create sentences, and others guess the missing word.

Sample Activity for Side by Side 1 page 99

a. Divide the class into pairs.

b. Give each pair a card with one of the following mystery words written on it:

nervous	tired	happy	cold
hungry	hot	angry	thirsty
sad	sick	embarrassed	

c. Have each pair create a sentence in which that word is in final position. For example:

   I'm biting my nails because I'm _____. (*nervous*)
   I shout at people when I'm _____. (*angry*)

d. One student from each pair then reads aloud the sentence with the final word missing. The other pairs of students try to guess the missing word.

Option: Do the activity as a game, in which each pair scores a point for identifying the correct mystery word. The pair with the most points wins the game.

47. *Pantomime Role Play*

Students act out role plays without speaking, and others guess the situation.

Sample Activity for Side by Side 1 pages 122–123

a. Make up role-play cards such as the following:

> A wife is upset. She and her husband are going to a concert, but her husband is still taking a shower. She doesn't want to be late.

> A mother is upset. She and her son are going to a baseball game, but her son is still sleeping. She doesn't want to be late.

> A husband is upset. He and his wife are going on a vacation, but his wife is still packing her suitcase. He doesn't want to be late for the plane.

b. Have pairs of students pantomime their role plays. The class watches and guesses the situation and what the two characters are saying.

48. *Pick-a-Sentence!*

Students form sentences by picking up word cards.

Sample Activity for Side by Side 1 pages 25-26

a. Write words from the lesson on separate word cards, mix up the cards, and put them in a pile on a desk or table in front of the room.

b. Have students take turns picking up one card at a time. (Students should keep all the cards they've picked.)

c. The object of the activity is to see how many sentences the class can pick. When someone has collected a group of cards that forms a sentence, that student should read it to the class to see if others agree that it's a correct sentence. If it's a sentence, have that student write it on the board.

d. The activity continues until all the cards have been picked.

Option: Do the activity as a game, with two competing teams. The team with the most sentences is the winner.

49. Picture Story

Sample Activity for Side by Side 2 pages 80-81

a. Put the following picture and word cues on the board:

Mr. Larson
cut himself
(swim)

Mrs. Larson
got seasick
(ride/boat)

Elizabeth
lost her glasses
(play football/beach)

Larry
hurt himself
(jog/beach)

Bobby
got a bad sunburn
(sleep/beach)

b. Point to the cues as you tell the following story: "Last month the Larson family had a terrible vacation in Hawaii. Mr. Larson cut himself while he was swimming. Mrs. Larson got seasick while she was riding on a boat. Their daughter Elizabeth lost her glasses while she was playing football on the beach. Their son Larry hurt himself while he was jogging. And their son Bobby got a bad sunburn while he was sleeping on the beach. The Larson family certainly had a terrible vacation!"

c. Call on pairs of students to ask and answer questions about the people in the story. For example:

    A. Where did the Larsons go for their vacation?
    B. They went to Hawaii.

    A. What happened to Mr. Larson?
    B. He cut himself while he was swimming.

d. Have students role-play characters in the story and tell what happened. Encourage students to expand the story, using any vocabulary they wish. For example:

    Mrs. Larson: While I was riding on a boat, I got seasick. Then I fainted!

50. Picture This!

Sample Activity for Side by Side 2 page 57

Describe a city street, and have students draw and label what you describe. For example:

> "This is First Avenue. There's a bank on First Avenue. Next to the bank on the left there's a supermarket. Across from the supermarket there's a cafeteria."
> (Etc.)

Option 1: Do the activity in pairs, where students take turns describing city streets.

Option 2: One student comes to the board, and the rest of the class gives instructions for that student to draw.

51. Question Game

Students create different questions based on the same sentence.

Sample Activity for Side by Side 3 pages 19-21

a. Write the following sentence on the board:

> Mrs. Watson went to Chicago last week.

b. Put a circle around different elements of the sentence, and have students create a question based on that portion of the sentence. For example:

> (Mrs. Watson) went to Chicago last week.

Who went to Chicago last week?

> Mrs. Watson went to Chicago (last week.)

When did Mrs. Watson go to Chicago?

> Mrs. Watson went to (Chicago) last week.

Where did Mrs. Watson go last week?

> Mrs. Watson (went to Chicago) last week.

What did Mrs. Watson do last week?

c. Continue with other sentences.

52. Question the Answers!

Students are given the answers and must create the appropriate questions.

Sample Activity for Side by Side 3 pages 62-63

a. Dictate answers such as the following to the class:

> For two hours.
> Since last week.
> For several years.
> Since I was a child.
> For twenty minutes.

b. Have students write questions for which these answers would be correct. For example:

> For two hours.   How long have you been waiting for the doctor?
> Since last week. How long has your back been hurting you?

c. Have students compare their questions with each other.

Option: Write the answers on cards. Divide the class into groups and give each group a set of cards.

53. Ranking

Students rank a list of vocabulary words.

Sample Activity for Side by Side 2 pages 96–97

a. Dictate the following food items to the class:

potato chips	butter	fruit
fish	rice	cheese
vegetables	eggs	chocolate cake
meat		

b. Have students rank these food items from the *healthiest* to the *unhealthiest*, with the first being the *healthiest*.

c. As a class, in pairs, or in small groups, have students compare their lists.

54. *Realia*

Students discuss real-world items brought to class.

Sample Activity for Side by Side 2 page 19

a. Cut out several supermarket advertisements from the newspaper and bring them to class.

b. Divide the class into pairs or small groups.

c. Have students compare the prices of the same food items in different supermarkets.

Sample Activity for Side by Side 2 page 63

a. Bring to class a few copies of a map of your city.

b. Divide the class into groups.

c. Have students ask and answer questions about how to get to various places in the community.

55. *Same and Different*

Students interview each other to learn ways in which they're the same and ways in which they're different.

VARIATION 1: SENTENCE COMPLETION

Sample Activity for Side by Side 1 page 92

a. Put the following on the board:

> I _____.
> He _____.
> She _____.
> We both _____.

b. Write a list of questions such as the following on the board or on a handout for students:

> Where are you from?
> Where do you live now?
> What language do you speak?
> How many brothers and sisters do you have?
> What do you usually have for breakfast?
> What newspaper do you usually read?

c. Divide the class into pairs.

d. Have students interview each other and then report to the class about the ways in which they're the *same* and the ways in which they're *different*. For example:

> I'm from Japan.
> Marta is from Colombia.
>
> I live in Centerville.
> She lives in Greenville.
>
> I speak Japanese.
> She speaks Spanish.
> We both speak English.
>
> I have two sisters.
> She has four brothers.
>
> We both have eggs for breakfast.
>
> I read the Daily Times.
> She reads the Daily Globe.

VARIATION 2: CATEGORIES

Sample Activity for Side by Side 3 page 121

a. Write the following categories on the board:

sports	school
music	home
food	family
clothes	travel

b. Divide the class into pairs.

c. The object is for pairs of students to find one thing in each of the categories that they have in common and then report back to the class. For example:

sports:	He can play tennis, and so can I.
music:	I like classical music, and he does, too.
food:	He ate cereal for breakfast, and so did I.
clothes:	I have a yellow raincoat, and he does, too.
school:	He enjoys science, and so do I.
home:	My apartment building has six floors, and his does, too.
family:	I have a cat and a dog, and so does he.
travel:	He's been to New York City, and so have I.

(continued)

a. Write the following categories on the board:

sports	school
music	home
food	family
clothes	travel

b. Divide the class into pairs.

c. The object is for pairs of students to find one thing in each of the categories that they *don't* have in common and then report back to the class. For example:

music:	I like rock music, but she doesn't.
food:	She enjoys Italian food, but I don't.
clothes:	Her shoes are red, but mine aren't.
school:	I'm taking history this year, but she isn't.
home:	My apartment has a jacuzzi, but hers doesn't.
family:	Her sister is in college, but mine isn't.
travel:	She's never flown in an airplane, but I have.

56. Scrambled Sentences

Students put words in the correct order to form sentences.

Sample Activity for Side by Side 2 page 69

a. Divide the class into two teams.

b. Write individual sentences out of order on the board. For example:

I'll	early	to	if	sleep	tired	I'm	go	
it	tomorrow	go	rains	if	movie	a	I'll	to
she	go	work	feels	if	to	back	better	she'll

c. The first person to raise his or her hand, come to the board, and write the sentence in the correct order earns a point for that team.

d. The team with the most points wins the scrambled sentence game.

Option: Write the words to several sentences on separate cards. Divide the class into small groups, and have students work together to put the sentences into correct order.

57. Scrambled Story

Students put sentences of a story in the correct order.

Sample Activity for Side by Side 1 page 138

Here is the story *Peter's Terrible Day*.

Peter went to a party last night.
He got up very late this morning.
He missed the train.
He had to walk to work.
He arrived at work at 10 o'clock.
His boss was very angry.
Peter had a headache all afternoon.

a. Write each sentence on a strip of paper. Then cut the words apart. Mix up the words in each sentence and clip them together.

b. Divide the class into small groups. Give each group one sentence to unscramble.

c. When everyone has put the words in correct order, have one student from each group write that group's sentence on the board.

d. Once all the sentences are on the board, have students decide what the correct order should be in order to tell the story *Peter's Terrible Day*.

Option: Instead of having students write the sentences on the board, have one student from each group come to the front of the room and say the sentence aloud. The class should then decide what the correct order is and tell the students to line up accordingly and retell the story.

58. Sense or Nonsense?

Students put together parts of sentences and decide if they *make sense* or are *nonsense.*

Sample Activity for Side by Side 1 pages 118–119

a. Divide the class into four groups.

b. Make four sets of split sentence cards with beginnings and endings of sentences. For example:

She's going to wash . . .	her car.
I'm going to visit . . .	my grandfather.
He's going to paint . . .	his living room.
We're going to play . . .	baseball.
I'm going to iron . . .	my pants.
She going to cut . . .	her hair.
They're going to go to . . .	the beach.
I going to fix . . .	my car.
They're going to plant . . .	flowers.
He's going to go . . .	skating.

c. Mix up the cards and distribute sets of cards to each group, keeping the beginning and ending cards in different piles.

d. Have students take turns picking up one card from each pile and reading the sentence to the group. For example:

I'm going to iron . . .	my car.

e. That group decides if the sentence makes *sense* or is *nonsense*.

59. Sentence Cues

Students make sentences based on key words.

Sample Activity for Side by Side 1 page 91

a. On separate cards, write key words that can be put together to form sentences. Clip together the cards for each sentence. For example:

I	speak	grandparents	every weekend
My sister	talk	boyfriend	every day
Our boss	never	say hello	us
Alan and Tom	rarely	study	library
Richard	read	newspaper	every morning
Our neighbor's dog	always	bark	night

b. Divide the class into small groups and give a clipped set of cards to each group.

c. Have each group write a sentence based on their set of cards.

d. Have one member of each group write that group's sentence on the board and compare everybody's sentences.

60. Sentences Alive!

Students hold up word cards and stand in line to make sentences.

Sample Activity for Side by Side 1 pages 42–44

a. Make up several sentences based on this lesson. For example:

>   My daughter is playing soccer in the park.
>   My wife is standing in front of our apartment building.
>   My husband is swimming at the beach.
>   My son is sitting on a bench and feeding the birds.
>   My grandparents are sitting on the sofa and watching TV.
>   My wife's brother is painting his living room.
>   My friends are dancing at my birthday party.

b. Write the words to each of these sentences on separate cards.

c. One sentence at a time, distribute the cards randomly to students in the class.

d. Have students decide on the correct word order of the sentence and then come to the front of the room. Have students make the sentence *come alive* by standing in order while holding up their cards and saying the sentence aloud one word at a time.

61. Sequencing

Sample Activity for Side by Side 3 page 12

a. Dictate the following sentences to students:

> He was late for an important meeting.
> Then he quickly ate breakfast and left the house.
> He took a shower and got dressed.
> He arrived at work at ten o'clock.
> He took the bus to the office.
> Henry got up late this morning.

b. Have students then sequence these sentences from one to six, with one being the first thing that happened to Henry:

1. Henry got up late this morning.
2. He took a shower and got dressed.
3. Then he quickly ate breakfast and left the house.
4. He took the bus to the office.
5. He arrived at work at ten o'clock.
6. He was late for an important meeting.

c. As a class, in pairs, or in small groups, have students compare their sequences.

62. Student-Led Dictation

Students take turns dictating short sentences to the class.

This activity is appropriate for any Side by Side lesson.

a. Tell each student to write down a short sentence based on the lesson in the book and look at it very carefully.

b. Have students take turns dictating their sentences to the class. Everybody writes down that student's sentence.

c. When the dictation is completed, call on different students to write each sentence on the board.

d. Have the class comment on the correctness of the sentences.

63. Survey

Students conduct surveys in class or in the community and report the results.

Sample Activity for Side by Side 2 page 99

a. Have students interview each other for advice on how to lose weight.

b. Have students report back to the class about their interviews.

Option: Have students also interview friends and family members and report to the class.

64. Telephone

Students take turns whispering phrases to each other.

Sample Activity for Side by Side 2 page 56

a. Divide the class into large groups. Have each group sit in a circle.

b. Whisper a set of directions to one student. For example:

"Walk up Main Street. The shoe store is on the right, next to the barber shop."

c. The first student whispers the directions to the second student, and so forth around the circle. The student listening may ask for clarification by saying, "I'm sorry. Could you repeat that?"

d. When the message gets to the last student, that person says it aloud. Is it the same message you started with? The group with the most accurate message wins.

65. Tell a Story!

Tell a short story to the class, and ask students questions about it.

Sample Activity for Side by Side 3 pages 19–21

a. Tell the following short story to the class:

> "Mr. and Mrs. Lane took a vacation last month. They went to Paris. They took the plane, but it was a terrible experience. The plane left three hours late, and they had very bad weather during the flight. When they arrived in Paris, it was raining. In fact, it rained for three days. They stayed in a small hotel and tried to eat in restaurants that weren't too expensive. They visited the Eiffel Tower and other famous places in Paris, they bought a few souvenirs, and they took a lot of photographs. They sent postcards to all their friends and told them about their trip. Mr. and Mrs. Lane didn't meet a lot of people because they didn't speak any French. But they didn't care. They had a very nice time."

b. After you finish telling the story, make several statements about it. Some should be true, and others should be false.

c. Students listen to the statements and decide if they're true or false. If a statement is false, have students correct it. For example:

> Teacher: Mr. and Mrs. Lane went to Madrid.
> Student: False. They didn't go to Madrid. They went to Paris.

Option: This activity can be done as a game with two competing teams. The teams take turns deciding whether the statements are true or false.

66. Tic Tac Definitions

Students play a *tic tac toe* game based on definitions.

Sample Activity for Side by Side 2 page 37

a. Have students draw a tic tac grid on their papers and fill in the grid with any nine of the nouns from the exercises on pages 36 or 37.

b. Give definitions of the words, and tell students to cross out any word on their grids for which you have given the definition.

c. The first person to cross out three words in a straight line—either vertically, horizontally, or diagonally—wins the game.

d. Have the winner call out the words to check the accuracy.

67. Tic Tac Grammar

Students play a *tic tac toe* game based on a grammar structure.

Sample Activity for Side by Side 3 pages 36-37

a. Have students draw a tic tac grid on a piece of paper and fill it in with the following verbs:

buy	see
eat	swim
give	take
get	wear
go	

b. Call out the past participle of any of these verbs. Tell students to cross out any present tense verb on their grid for which you have given a past participle form.

c. The first person to cross out three verbs in a straight line—either vertically, horizontally, or diagonally—wins the game.

d. Have the winner call out the words to check the accuracy.

Sample Activity for Side by Side 2 page 19

a. Have students draw a tic tac grid and fill it in with any nine of the following words:

bag	head
bottle	jar
box	loaf
bunch	pound
can	quart
dozen	

b. Call out the name of a food item. If a student has written on his or her grid a container or quantity that the item comes in, the student should write "of" and the name of the item in the appropriate box. For example: *butter*.

box	jar	head
loaf	bunch	quart
bottle	bag	pound *of butter*

c. The first student to write in three items in a straight line—either vertically, horizontally or diagonally—wins the game.

d. Have the winner call out the words to check for accuracy.

68. Tic Tac Question Formation

Students play a *tic tac toe* game in which they form questions based on key words.

Sample Activity for Side by Side 1 page 87

a. Draw a tic tac grid on the board and fill it with question words. For example:

When?	Who?	Is there?
What?	How many?	Where?
What kind?	Are there?	Which?

b. Divide the class into two teams. Give each team a mark: X or O.

c. Have each team ask a question that begins with one of the question words and then provide the answer to the question. If the question and answer are correct, the team gets to put its mark in that space. For example:

X Team: What kind of books do you like?
I like novels.

When?	Who?	Is there?
What?	How many?	Where?
X	Are there?	Which?

d. The first team to mark out three boxes in a straight line—either vertically, horizontally, or diagonally—wins.

69. Tic Tac Question the Answer

> Students play a *tic tac toe* game in which they form questions based on answers.

Sample Activity for Side by Side 3 page 41

a. Draw a tic tac grid on the board and fill it in with short answers to questions:

Yes, we have.	No, she hasn't.	Yes, he did.
No, I didn't.	Yes, I have.	No, it hasn't.
No, they haven't.	Yes, he has.	No, we didn't.

b. Divide the class into teams. Give each team a mark: X or O.

c. Have each team ask a question for an answer in the grid. For example:

> X Team: Have you done your homework yet?
> Yes, I have.

d. If an answer is appropriate and is stated correctly, that team may replace the answer with its team mark. For example:

Yes, we have.	No, she hasn't.	Yes, he did.
No, I didn't.	**X**	No, it hasn't.
No, they haven't.	Yes, he has.	No, we didn't.

e. The first team to mark out three boxes in a straight line—either vertically, horizontally or diagonally—wins.

70. Tic Tac Vocabulary

> **Students play a *tic tac toe* game based on vocabulary items.**

Sample Activity for Side by Side 1 page 34–35

a. Have students draw a tic tac grid on their papers and then fill in their grids with any nine of the following adjectives:

married	expensive
small	pretty
short	difficult
young	thin
poor	quiet

b. Tell students that you're going to say the *opposites* of the words in their grids. So when they hear a word, they should look for the opposite of that word and cross it out.

c. The first person to cross out three opposites in a straight line—either vertically, horizontally, or diagonally—wins the game.

d. Have the winner call out the words to check the accuracy.

Sample Activity for Side by Side 1 page 98

a. Have students draw a tic tac grid and fill it in with the following words:

hungry	angry
cold	sick
tired	hot
embarrassed	nervous
thirsty	

b. Say the beginnings of the following sentences and tell students to cross out the word that finishes each sentence:

I always shiver when I'm . . .
I'm shouting because I'm . . .
I always blush when I'm . . .
I'm going to the doctor because I'm . . .
I always bite my nails when I'm . . .
I'm drinking because I'm . . .
I'm eating because I'm . . .
I always perspire when I'm . . .
I'm yawning because I'm . . .

c. The first student to cross out three words in a straight line—either vertically, horizontally, or diagonally—wins the game.

d. Have the winner call out the words to check for accuracy.

71. Time Line

Sample Activity for Side by Side 1 page 149

a. Put the following time line on the board:

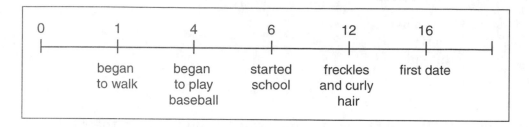

b. Tell about that person. For example:

> Carla began to walk when she was one year old.
> When she was four years old, she began to play baseball.
> She started school when she was six years old.
> When she was twelve years old, she had freckles and curly hair.
> She went on her first date when she was sixteen years old.

c. Ask questions about the time line. For example:

> When did Carla begin to walk?
> How old was she when she started school?

d. Call on pairs of students to ask and answer questions about the time line.

e. Have students make a time line based on their own lives and then talk about it in pairs or small groups.

72. True or False?

Sample Activity for Side by Side 1 page 65

a. Bring in pictures from magazines, newspapers, or mail order catalogs that depict clothing items.

b. Make statements about the pictures and have students tell you "true" or "false." If the statement is false, have students correct it.

Option: You can call on students to make true or false statements about the visuals and have other students respond.

73. True or False Memory Game

Students try to remember details of a picture they've just seen.

Sample Activity for Side by Side 4 pages 24–25

a. Find a picture from a magazine and show it to the class for one minute. The picture should depict a scene that lends itself to being described with several adjectives.

b. Put the picture away, and then make several statements about the picture, using adjectives. The statements may be true or false.

c. Students have to decide if each statement is true or false.

d. Then have students look at the picture to see if they were right.

Option: This can be done as a dictation with a *True* column and a *False* column. Tell students to write each statement in the appropriate column. At the end of the dictation, have students check the picture to see if they were correct.

74. What Came Before?

Students create dialogs based on just the final line.

Sample Activity for Side by Side 4 pages 52-53

a. Divide the class into pairs.

b. Write on the board the final line of a conversation. For example:

> I don't believe it! She could have had a terrible accident!

Other possible final lines:

> That's terrible! He could have gotten hurt!
> I don't believe it! They could have gotten sick!
> You're kidding! You could have wound up in jail!

c. Have each pair create a conversation ending with that line.

d. Call on pairs to present their conversations to the class and compare everybody's versions.

Option: Have students continue their conversations to see what happens next.

75. What's Wrong?

Give students incorrect sentences and have them correct them.

Sample Activity for Side by Side 3 pages 52–53

a. Divide the class into pairs or small groups.

b. Write several sentences such as the following on the board or on a handout. Some of the sentences should be correct, and others incorrect. For example:

> I know them for a long time.
> He's been interested in computers since many years.
> She's played the piano since she was a child.
> They been married for fifty years.
> How long you own that car?
> I been sick since last Monday.
> You've had a backache for a week.
> How long there be problems at your company?

c. The object of the activity is for students to identify which sentences are incorrect and then correct them.

d. Have students compare their answers.

Option: Do the activity as a game, with competing teams. The team that successfully completes the task in the shortest time is the winner.

76. Which One Isn't True?

Students make several true statements about themselves and one false one. The class must guess which one isn't true.

Sample Activity for Side by Side 3 pages 68–69

a. Tell students to write three true statements and one false statement about themselves. For example:

> I've never given blood.
> I've run in several marathons.
> I called the president on the telephone last week.
> I've been studying Swahili for the past two years.

b. Have students take turns reading their statements to the class and have the class guess which statement isn't true.

OVERVIEW OF COMMUNICATION ACTIVITIES

1. Ask Me a Question! *(Page 1)*
Students ask each other questions to guess a *mystery* person, place, thing, or action.

2. Associations *(Page 2)*
Students brainstorm associations.

3. Beanbag Toss *(Page 2)*
Students call out vocabulary items while tossing a beanbag to each other.

Students call out short sentences while tossing a beanbag to each other.

4. Bleep! *(Page 3)*
Students create dialogs containing hidden words.

5. Board Game *(Page 4)*
Students play a board game in which they answer questions.

6. Build Your Vocabulary! *(Page 5)*
Students keep a record of new words they encounter outside of class.

7. Can You Hear the Difference? *(Page 5)*
Students discriminate between similar sounding words or sentences.

8. Category Dictation *(Page 6)*
Establish columns for different vocabulary or grammatical categories. Dictate words and have students write them under the appropriate category.

9. Chain Game *(Page 7)*
Students extend a sentence by adding more and more vocabulary items.

10. Chain Story *(Page 7)*
Students create a story by adding one new sentence at a time.

11. Change the Sentence! *(Page 8)*
Students make changes to sentences, one portion at a time.

12. Clap in Rhythm *(Page 8)*
Students call out vocabulary items while clapping their hands.

13. Class Discussion *(Page 9)*
Students discuss situations presented in the text.

14. Class Story *(Page 9)*
Students develop a story based on a situation from the text.

15. Concentration *(Page 10)*
Students match corresponding vocabulary items or grammar constructions.

16. Conversation Framework *(Page 12)*
Students use a dialog framework for talking about their experiences.

17. Correct the Statement! *Page 13)*
Students correct incorrect statements.

18. Describe the Picture! *(Page 14)*
Students describe pictures designed to elicit specific vocabulary or grammar structures.

19. Dialog Builder! *(Page 14)*
Give students a line from a dialog and have them create a conversation incorporating that line.

20. Dictate and Discuss *(Page 15)*
Dictate sentences and have students discuss them.

21. Dictation Game *(Page 15)*
Pairs of students dictate sentences to each other.

22. Do You Remember? *(Page 16)*
Students try to remember what they saw in a picture.

23. Draw, Write, and Read *(Page 16)*
Students draw and write descriptions.

24. Drawing Game *(Page 17)*
Students draw vocabulary words for others to guess.

25. Expand the Sentence! *(Page 18)*
Students take turns adding words to expand a sentence.

26. Find the Right Person! *(Page 18)*
Students have information about others in the class and interview each other to identify the correct people.

27. Finish the Sentence! *(Page 20)*
Students complete sentences with appropriate vocabulary words.

28. Finish the Sentence Line-Up *(Page 21)*
Students line up opposite each other and complete sentences.

29. Grammar Chain *(Page 22)*
Students do a chain game exercise with a grammatical focus.

30. Group Story *(Page 22)*
Groups of students create stories which they retell to the class.

31. Guess the Word! *(Page 23)*
Students try to guess a word by asking yes/no questions.

32. How Many Questions? *(Page 23)*
Give students answers to questions and have them try to create as many questions for that answer as they can.

33. How Many Sentences? *(Page 24)*
Students make up sentences based on a group of words.

34. In Your Opinion *(Page 25)*
Students express their opinions based on content of the textbook lesson.

35. Information Gap Handouts *(Page 26)*
Pairs of students compare different information.

36. Information Gap Role Play *(Page 27)*
Students create role plays in which each student has different information.

37. Information Search *(Page 28)*
Students look for answers to questions and report back to the class.

38. Interview *(Page 28)*
Students interview each other and report back to the class.

39. Key Word Role Play *(Page 28)*
Students create role plays incorporating key words and structures from the lesson.

40. Letter Game *(Page 29)*
Students guess vocabulary items based on the first letter.

41. Match the Conversations *(Page 30)*
Students match sentences with their appropriate rejoinders.